CAN WE HELP?

KIDS VOLUNTEERING TO HELP THEIR COMMUNITIES

George Ancona

CANDLEWICK PRESS

First edition 2015

Library of Congress Catalog Card Number 2014951417
ISBN 978-0-7636-7367-3

15 16 17 18 19 20 APS 10 9 8 7 6 5 4 3 2 1

Printed in Humen, Dongguan, China

This book was typeset in Maiandra.

Candlewick Press
99 Dover Street
Somerville, Massachusetts 02144

visit us at www.candlewick.com

Can
We
Help
?

Of course you can!

You can help your family, a neighbor, or even someone you don't know. If someone is hungry, you can get him some food. If someone is cold, you can make her a hat or scarf. If someone is lonely, you can read him a story.

You can help or volunteer alone, with a friend, or with your family. There are whole groups of people that help people in need! You can volunteer with one of these groups to help others. Helping people will make you feel good.

People who are homeless need shelter, food, and clothing. Farms, stores, religious organizations, and schools often donate food and clothing to shelters. These students are knitting hats and scarves for homeless families and others in need.

To make hats, the students use round plastic knitting looms and colorful yarn. To knit scarves, Amelia uses just part of a loom and Sara uses straight knitting needles.

Each hat or scarf takes about a week to make. Jack stretches his scarf to see how long it is. When Campbell is finished knitting his hat, he tries it on. Then all the students put on their creations, happy that their handiwork will help keep someone warm.

A community farm grows produce to give to organizations that help feed people who don't have enough to eat. Men, women, and children volunteer their time to plant, grow, and harvest fruits and vegetables.

At harvesttime, families are invited to pick the produce. Children work alongside the grown-ups as they move up and down the rows of plants.

Soon hundreds of tomatoes, carrots, squash, beets, peppers, strawberries, and other fruits and vegetables fill the crates and wheelbarrows in the fields.

Dominic and his mom wash the fresh carrots. Later, the produce will be sent to soup kitchens and shelters in town.

The Food Depot is a place that collects food donated by growers, supermarkets, and stores. They have a huge cold warehouse where they store donations and pack them up to distribute.

They invite families to come pack plastic bags with food. These bags are then given to people who don't have enough to eat.

The kids pick plums from huge cardboard tubs. Each child picks eight plums and puts them into a bag. Katelyn finds a bad plum and throws it into a separate barrel.

The bags are put into cardboard boxes. They'll be delivered to organizations where hungry people can come to get them. Schools will give the bags to children who need food at home.

To celebrate a job well done, the kids cover the empty tub and make a drum to pound on.

On another day, volunteers pack bags of donated snacks for schoolkids. These are given to children whose parents are not home when they return from school. With these donations, the kids will be sure to have snacks in the afternoon.

Elan unpacks one of the many cartons of donated snacks. There are several different kinds. She chooses one of each and puts them into a bag.

Rosie helps by tying a knot in each bag.
Elena then packs the bags into the cartons
that will be sent to schools.

The girls work together to seal and label the cartons. Then they lift each box onto a pallet. Later, a forklift will take the cartons into the refrigerated warehouse.

Elena dances in a costume she created out of some empty cartons.

Kitchen Angels is an organization that provides hot meals for folks who can't cook for themselves. The meals are cooked by volunteers and then packed into separate shopping bags for each person. The bags are put in an insulated box to keep them warm until they are delivered.

Volunteers pick up the bags to deliver them to people in town. All the volunteers sign in when they arrive to pick up the meals. Molly and her dad are volunteers who deliver meals. She is six years old and has been volunteering for two years.

It is dark and cold when Molly and her dad deliver a meal to Mr. Louis, who doesn't see too well. He looks forward to greeting Molly and getting his dinner.

During the winter holidays, children and grown-ups gather to wrap gifts for the people who receive meals from Kitchen Angels. Phin works with Mr. Moore. On the other side of the crowded room, Kyle and his brother Carlos wrap small gifts alongside their mom.

Samantha ties a pretty
ribbon around a gift.
This week the volunteers
will deliver the Christmas
gifts with the dinners.

Specially trained dogs can help people who have physical or mental disabilities. Puppies start their training to be assistance dogs when they are just two months old. It takes about two years to train a dog.

At first, assistance dogs are trained by professional adult trainers. Then school-children volunteer to give the dogs the experience of hearing young voices giving commands. The dogs will learn about ninety words, beginning with their own names.

Anna is a trainer who brings the dogs to a local school. She begins a class by pairing up each dog with a student. She tries to match a frisky dog with an active student or a timid dog with a shy student. That student becomes the dog's trainer, and they become a team.

Alex and Serena start the class by strapping bags of treats to their waists. These are the rewards they will give to their dogs when they do the right thing. Ulysses is paired with a black Labrador retriever named Olivia. Each student spends the beginning of the class talking to, scratching, and patting his or her dog.

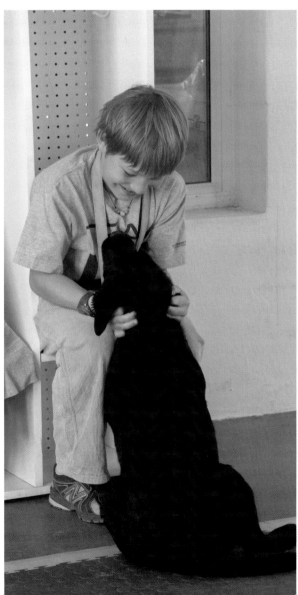

Alex brushes Hubbard's teeth and then hugs him. Meanwhile, Max brushes Blossom's coat. They learn commands like *sit*, *wait*, *go to bed*, *left*, *right*, *drop it*, *bring it here*, and many others.

Henry teaches Hula to open a door by pressing a switch with her nose.

Sophia gives Tahiti a treat when she responds to her command: *down*.

Each dog is kept on a leash so that it will stay close to its trainer. An assistance dog must be able to walk with its owner into supermarkets and stores to shop. Uli trains Riley from a wheelchair to get Riley used to moving with it.

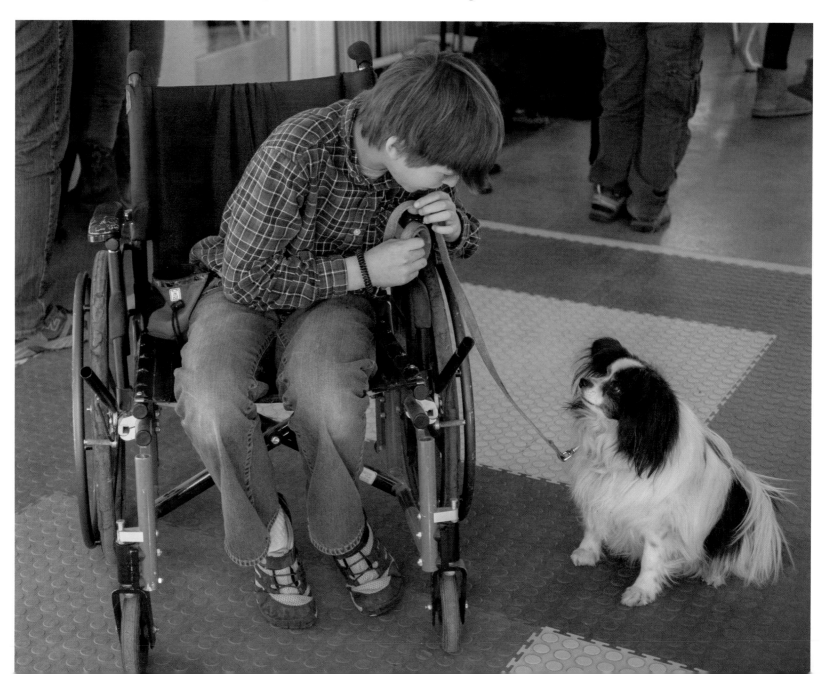

Geneva walks Hubbard through the building. Next they practice walking around the playing field. Each dog-and-trainer pair moves, sits, or lies down . . . together.

During the training, the dogs are introduced to people who need assistance. At that time, it is the dog that chooses the person it will spend the rest of its life with. At graduation, the dog is handed over by the student trainer to the new partner.

Some volunteers help people with physical disabilities ski on a snowy mountain. Gavyn and his dad have been doing this for several years.

They help people like Mike, who gets around in a wheelchair. On winter Saturdays, Mike's parents bring him to the mountain. They and Gavyn lift him from his wheelchair into a bi-ski and strap him in. Then Gavyn, an adult instructor, and Mike ride the chairlift together.

At the top of the slope, Gavyn steers using the handles behind Mike. The instructor holds on to two long belts for safety. Off they go, making turns from side to side all the way down the slope amid the other skiers.

After an hour and a half and many trips down the slopes, Mike and Gavyn are all smiles.

It's almost spring. Two years ago, this town planted shrubs along a river. The roots from the shrubs help to hold the soil in place and keep it from washing away. Gio and his dad, Leonardo, planted a hundred cottonwood trees along the banks in their neighborhood.

But some years the river runs dry because of drought. The young trees don't get enough water, even when the local reservoir releases some water that flows downriver.

Gio, his dad, Ciela, Felix, Oliver, Zubin, and Wyatt gather at the river with buckets and plastic jugs to scoop up water from the river. They carry the full buckets to the thirsty trees and pour the water into a well around the base of each tree.

When Ciela pours her bucket of water into the well, the water begins to bubble. The soil is soaking up the water. The young crew works its way along the river until all the saplings have been watered.

A playful rock-throwing contest takes place before they go home for lunch. After about three weeks, cottonwood buds begin to pop out on the delicate branches. The trees have survived the drought, and spring has arrived in the neighborhood for all to enjoy.

Some schools have a mentorship program. The middle-school students shown here volunteer to help elementary students with their studies. Once a week after school, young students are dropped off at the middle school, where the older students meet them.

They gather in a drama room, which has costumes hanging against the wall, with hats and helmets on a shelf above. There are also drums, exercise balls, and other props around the room.

Jennifer, the teacher, plays a game that helps the two groups get
to know each other. Once they have learned one another's names,
the young students are paired up with the older mentors.

Emma tutors Kiara. Lucinda works with Julian.

Graham is with Laila. Dominica helps Lucas.

The younger students get help with their writing and mathematics homework. Then they read books and talk about the stories. They also play word games.

At five o'clock, it's time to go home—but not before some last moments
of fun. Graham puts on a bonnet from the shelf and takes a turn beating
a drum. They all look forward to next week.

This Boys and Girls Club has adopted the road leading to their clubhouse. It's a beautiful environment, with snow-covered mountains in the background. Once a month, a crew of kid volunteers hits the road to pick up the trash that people have tossed out of their cars. They find cans, bottles, bags, wrappers, and all sorts of junk.

The kid volunteers gather in the clubhouse to get gloves and black trash bags. Then they fan out on either side of the road. Some of the kids walk in the deep gullies where trash rolls down. Others stay close to the pavement.

Most of the small trash is tossed into bags. Whenever a big object is found, it is shown off as a prize. After about an hour, the friends reach the end of the road, where a sign names their club. A shout of jubilation pierces the air. The bus takes them with their full black bags back to the club.

THANK YOU
PUEBLO OF POJOAQUE
BOYS AND GIRLS
CLUB

For helping to keep this segment of road
litter-free

SANTA FE COUNTY
ADOPT-A-ROAD
PROGRAM

Acknowledgments

I'd like to thank the various organizations, schools, parents, teachers, coordinators, children, and friends in Santa Fe, New Mexico, who invited me into their worlds: Kristen Mitchell of the **Rio Grande School,** along with her second-graders;
Roy Stephenson of **The Community Farm;**
Jill Gentry of **The Food Depot;**
Lauren LaVail of **Kitchen Angels;**
Linda Milanesi, Anna Wilder, and Jodie Backensto of **Assistance Dogs of the West;**
La Mariposa Montessori School;
Gavyn and Stuart Pendleton of the **Adaptive Ski Program;**
Gio and Leonardo Segura;
Perli Cunanan and Jennifer Love of the **Santa Fe School for the Arts and Sciences;**
Donald Christy and Andrea Gallego of the **Pueblo of Pojoaque Boys & Girls Club.**
Thanks as well to Sue McDonald, who researched sources, and to Molly Bradbury and Michelle Eckhardt, my technical assistants on this, my first digital-photography project.

Author's Note

I grew up during the Depression. Once, my dad was out of a job and wasn't able to pay our fifteen-dollar rent. So the landlord came and moved us out of the apartment onto the street during winter—my dad, my mom, my kid sister, and me.

When the neighbors saw this, they all chipped in to pay our rent and moved us back in.

That's why when my editor, Hilary Van Dusen, asked me to do this book, I said yes. I wanted to show some of the ways kids can volunteer to help their neighbors and community . . . and the fun they can have doing it.